LEGO Legends of CHIMA

TRIBES OF CHIMA™

WRITTEN BY
RUTH AMOS

DK DELHI
Assistant Editor Gaurav Joshi
Senior Editor Garima Sharma
Art Editor Anamica Roy
Deputy Managing Art Editor Neha Ahuja
DTP Designer Umesh Singh Rawat, Sachin Singh
Pre-Production Manager Sunil Sharma

Reading Consultant
Maureen Fernandes

First published in 2014 in Great Britain by
Dorling Kindersley Limited
80 Strand, London, WC2R 0RL

10 9 8 7 6 5 4 3 2 1
001—196561—Jan/2014

Page design copyright © 2014 Dorling Kindersley Limited
LEGO, the LEGO logo, the Brick and Knob configurations, the Minifigure
and LEGENDS OF CHIMA are trademarks of the LEGO Group.
© 2014 The LEGO Group
Produced by Dorling Kindersley Limited under licence from the LEGO Group.

A CIP catalogue record for this book is
available from the British Library.

ISBN: 978-1-40934-682-1

Colour reproduction by Alta Image
Printed and bound in China by South China

Discover more at

www.dk.com
www.LEGO.com

Contents

Welcome to Chima™!

This is the land of Chima™.
Chima is a beautiful kingdom
with jungles, mountains
and rivers.

Many animals live here.
The animals have discovered
a magical energy source
called CHI.

WHAT IS CHI?

CHI is a magical source of energy.

ORB OF CHI

Where does CHI come from?

CHI flows down from the floating Mount Cavora.

It collects in the magical Sacred Pool.

What does CHI look like?

CHI looks like a ball of glowing, blue magical water.

MOUNT CAVORA

Who uses CHI?

All animals in Chima use CHI.

Why do animals use CHI?

Animals can walk and talk like humans when they use CHI. They can also build, invent and power their vehicles.

7

The Animal Tribes

Long ago, the animals in
Chima walked on four legs.
Some of the animals drank
CHI and started to walk
on two legs.

These animals make up tribes.
They are the Lion, Crocodile,
Eagle, Raven, Gorilla and
Wolf tribes.

V HICLES OF C IM

The tribes of Chima design their own special vehicles. Here are some of them.

NAME: Lion Attack
TRIBE: Lion
FEATURE: The powerful Lion Attack Vehicle can carry many missiles.

NAME: Claw Ripper
TRIBE: Crocodile
FEATURE:
The Ripper has a huge mouth that opens up to trap enemies.

NAME: Ultra Striker
TRIBE: Eagle
FEATURE: The Striker's front claws can crush anything in their way.

NAME: Combat Lair
TRIBE: Wolf
FEATURE: The Lair can split into a helicopter, two tricycles, a prison unit and a motorcycle.

NAME: CHI Raider
TRIBE: Raven
FEATURE: The CHI Raider has a special area at the back to store the CHI that the Ravens steal.

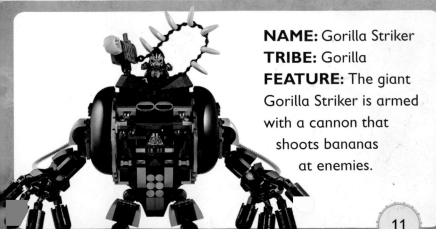

NAME: Gorilla Striker
TRIBE: Gorilla
FEATURE: The giant Gorilla Striker is armed with a cannon that shoots bananas at enemies.

The Lion Tribe

The Lion Tribe is the
noblest tribe of all.
The Lions are the
guardians of the CHI.
They share it out with
all the other animals.
They are always very fair.
The Lions live in the
splendid Lion City.

Longtooth

Longtooth is an old foot
soldier in the Lion Tribe.
He has fought in many
battles, but now
he prefers talking
to fighting.

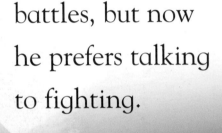

Laval

Flame-haired Laval is
brave, but he is headstrong.
One day he will be King
of the Lions.

The Crocodile Tribe

The Crocodiles
can be sneaky and
selfish. They look
scary, with tough,
scaly skin and
sharp teeth.
The crocodiles
live in forts in
the swamps.

Cragger

Cragger is the young prince
of the Crocodile Tribe.
Cragger is very greedy.
He wants to get his claws
on more CHI.

Crominus

King Crominus is the Crocodile
leader and Cragger's father.
Crominus is a tough ruler
who protects his tribe.

CRAGGER'S
COMMAND SHIP

Helicopter parked
at the back

Movable tail

Propellers

Small boats on
either side

Red cockpits look like fiery eyes

Movable mouth

Front claws

The Eagle Tribe

The Eagles are clever
and thoughtful.
They are always talking
about ideas.
They just really love thinking!

The Eagles pilot the
Eagle Interceptor.
They live high up on rocky cliffs.

Eris

Eris the Eagle loves
solving puzzles.
She is good at inventing
battle tactics, but she prefers
to avoid fighting.

Eglor

Eglor loves riding
his Speedor.
Here he is trying
to land it on a
treetop nest target.

SPEEDOR

Laval **VS.** **Worriz**

Gorda **VS.** **Crug**

See star racers go head to head!

RACE

TOMORROW

In The Grand Arena

Gates open at 6pm

27

The Raven Tribe

The Ravens are sly birds.
They love to steal,
even from
their friends.

The Ravens pilot a Glider.
They live in messy Nest Forts.
Nest Forts are like mazes inside.
It is best not to visit – you may
never find your way out!

Rizzo

Rizzo is the scruffiest Raven,
but he does not care.
He uses his Grabberatus
claw tool to steal CHI!

Rawzom

Rawzom is the
King of the Ravens.
He does not say much,
but when he does speak,
the Ravens obey him!

RAWZOM

LOVES:
To steal
weapons

**SPECIAL
FEATURE:**
Golden chest protector

**FAVOURITE
WEAPON:**
A spike shaped
like a beak

RAZAR

LOVES:
To be selfish

**SPECIAL
FEATURE:**
Left hand is
a silver hook

**FAVOURITE
WEAPON:**
A chainsaw with
a red blade

RAZCAL

LOVES:
To count
stolen goods

**SPECIAL
FEATURE:**
Golden beak

**FAVOURITE
WEAPON:**
A CHI-blaster with
two blades

RIZZO

LOVES:
To fight

**SPECIAL
FEATURE:**
Right peg leg

**FAVOURITE
WEAPON:**
A pulsar blaster

The Wolf Tribe

The Wolves are ferocious,
but they are also practical.
They roam around Chima
in a pack.
They live in
vehicles like this
Combat Lair.

The wolves squeeze into
the lair together, so life
is cramped and smelly!

Wilhurt

Wilhurt is a mean and
dangerous brute!
He spends all day stalking
prey with his big, black axe.

Winzar

Winzar is a young wolf
who is full of energy.
He loves to ride his
powerful Speedor.

The Gorilla Tribe

The Gorillas are
peace-loving creatures.
They may look
scary, but they are
gentle at heart.
However, when they
get angry, nobody
can defeat them.
The Gorillas pilot
a huge robot called
the Gorilla Striker.

Skinnet the Skunk

Skinnet is harmless, but he can be very smelly. Nobody wants to get too close to stinky Skinnet.

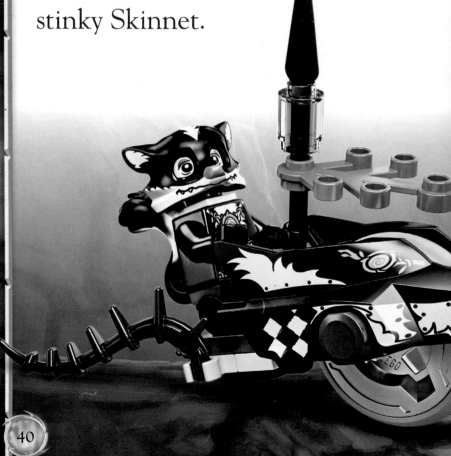

Furty the Fox

Furty is a sly and selfish fox. He will only be friends with someone if he gets something he wants in return.

Quiz

1. What is the colour of a CHI orb?

2. Where does CHI flow
down from?

3. What is this vehicle called?

4. Which tribe has tough scaly skin
and sharp teeth?

5. Who is Cragger's father?

6. Which member of the Eagle Tribe is this?

7. Who is the King of the Ravens?

8. Which animal tribe travels in a pack?

9. What does the Gorilla Striker shoot at enemies?

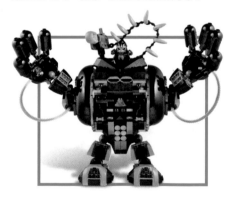

10. Who is the smelliest animal in Chima?

Answers on page 45

Glossary

ferocious someone who is scary and dangerous

guardian someone who looks after or protects something

headstrong someone who only does what he wants to do

invent create something new

selfish caring only about yourself

Speedor one-wheeled vehicle powered by CHI

tool device used to make work easier

Index

Answers to the quiz on pages 42 and 43:
1. Blue 2. From Mount Cavora 3. Lion Attack Vehicle
4. The Crocodile Tribe 5. King Crominus 6. Eris
7. Rawzom 8. The Wolf Tribe 9. Bananas
10. Skinnet the Skunk

Guide for Parents

DK Reads is a three-level reading series for children, developing the habit of reading widely for both pleasure and information. These books have exciting running text interspersed with a range of reading genres to suit your child's reading ability, as required by the school curriculum. Each book is designed to develop your child's reading skills, fluency, grammar awareness and comprehension in order to build confidence and engagement when reading.

Ready for a *Beginning to Read* book

YOUR CHILD SHOULD

- be using phonics, including combinations of consonants, such as bl, gl and sm, to read unfamiliar words; and common word endings, such as plurals, ing, ed and ly.
- be using the storyline, illustrations and the grammar of a sentence to check and correct their own reading.
- be pausing briefly at commas, and for longer at full stops; and altering his/her expression to respond to question, exclamation and speech marks.

A Valuable And Shared Reading Experience

For many children, reading requires much effort but adult participation can make this both fun and easier. So here are a few tips on how to use this book with your child.

TIP 1: Check out the contents together before your child begins:

- Read the text about the book on the back cover.
- Read through and discuss the contents page together to heighten your child's interest and expectation.
- Briefly discuss any unfamiliar or difficult words on the contents page.

- Chat about the non-fiction reading features used in the book, such as headings, captions, recipes, lists or charts.

This introduction helps to put your child in control and makes the reading challenge less daunting.

TIP 2: Support your child as he/she reads the story pages:

- Give the book to your child to read and turn the pages.

- Where necessary, encourage your child to break a word into syllables, sound out each one and then flow the syllables together. Ask him/her to reread the sentence to check the meaning.

- When there's a question mark or an exclamation mark, encourage your child to vary his/her voice as he/she reads the sentence. Demonstrate how to do this if it is helpful.

TIP 3: Praise, share and chat:

- The factual pages tend to be more difficult than the story pages, and are designed to be shared with your child.

- Ask questions about the text and the meaning of the words used. Ask your child to suggest his/her own quiz questions. These help to develop comprehension skills and awareness of the language used.

A FEW ADDITIONAL TIPS

- Try and read together everyday. Little and often is best. These books are divided into manageable chapters for one reading session. However after 10 minutes, only keep going if your child wants to read on.

- Always encourage your child to have a go at reading difficult words by themselves. Praise any self-corrections, for example, "I like the way you sounded out that word and then changed the way you said it, to make sense".

- Read other books of different types to your child just for enjoyment and information.

Here are some other DK Reads you might enjoy.

Beginning to Read

Pirate Attack!
Come and join Captain Blackbeard and his pirate crew for an action-packed adventure on the high seas.

Deadly Dinosaurs
Roar! Thud! Meet Rexy, Sid, Deano and Sonia, the museum dinosaurs that come alive at night.

Starting to Read Alone

The Great Panda Tale
Join the excitement at the zoo as the staff prepare to welcome a new panda baby.

Terrors of the Deep
Marine biologists Dom and Jake take their deep-sea submersible down into the deepest, darkest ocean trenches in the world.

Pony Club
Emma is so excited – she is going to horse-riding camp with her older sister!

LEGO® Friends: Summer Adventures
Enjoy a summer of fun in Heartlake City with Emma, Mia, Andrea, Stephanie, Olivia and friends.